For trans activists of all ages
JABL

*To Mark, for all your support
in making this book*
QL

First published 2021 by Walker Books Ltd
87 Vauxhall Walk, London SE11 5HJ

2 4 6 8 10 9 7 5 3 1

Text © 2021 JonArno Lawson
Illustrations © 2021 Qin Leng

The right of JonArno Lawson and Qin Leng to be identified as author and illustrator respectively of this work
has been asserted by them in accordance with the Copyright, Designs and Patents Act 1988

Printed in China

British Library Cataloguing in Publication Data:
a catalogue record for this book is available from the British Library

ISBN 978-1-4063-9667-6

www.walker.co.uk

OVER THE SHOP

JonArno Lawson   illustrated by Qin Leng

WALKER BOOKS
AND SUBSIDIARIES
LONDON · BOSTON · SYDNEY · AUCKLAND

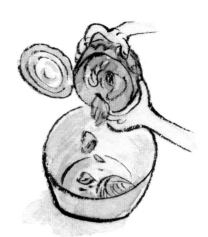

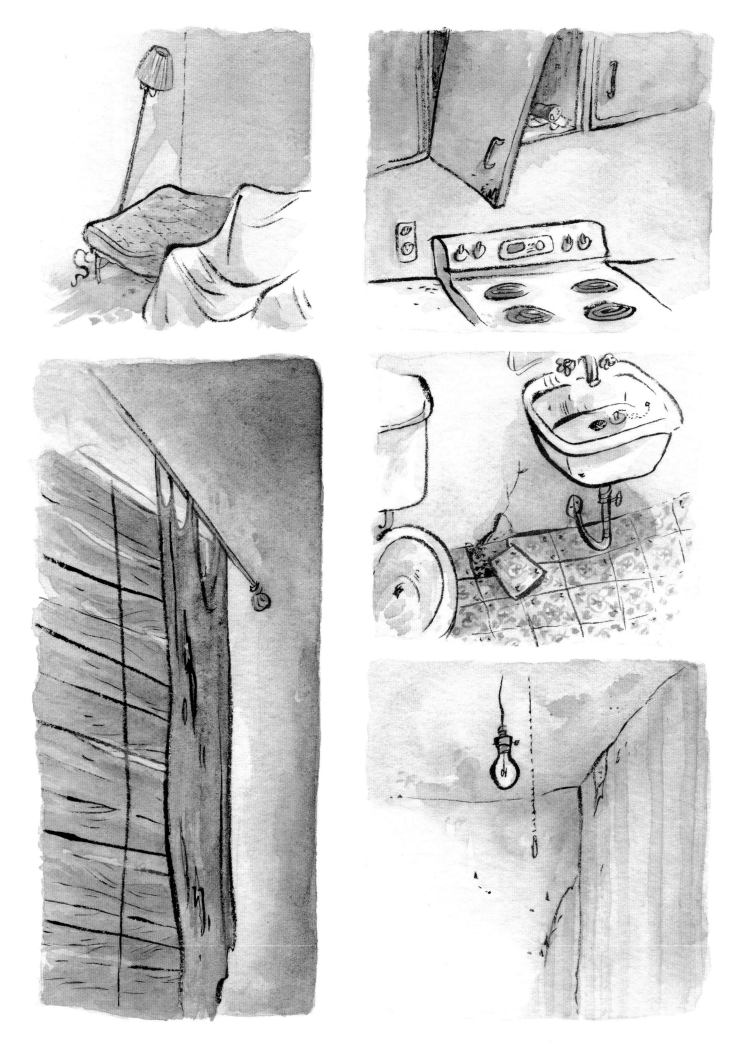